CONTENTS

I0878435

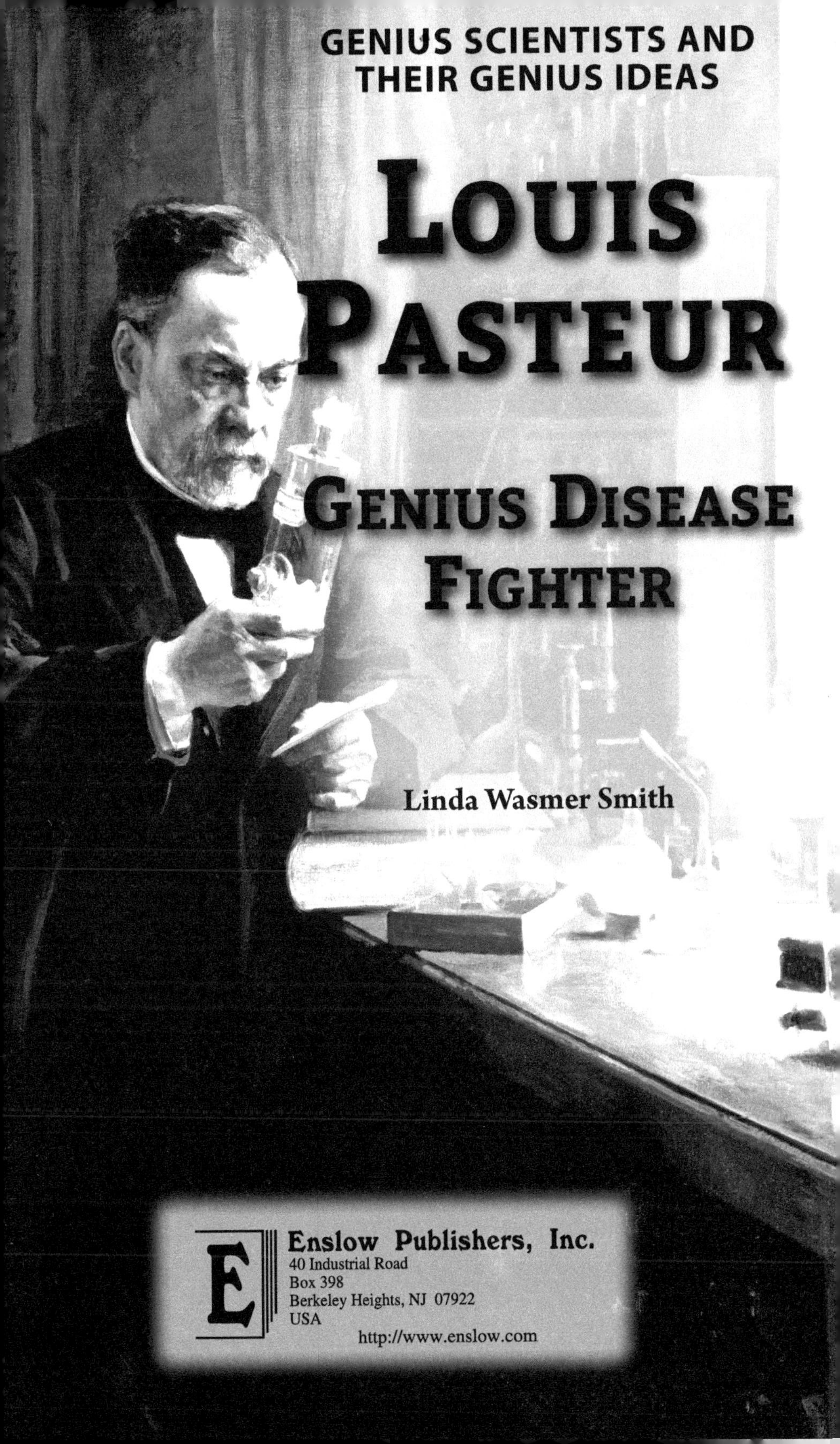

GENIUS SCIENTISTS AND THEIR GENIUS IDEAS

LOUIS PASTEUR

GENIUS DISEASE FIGHTER

Linda Wasmer Smith

Enslow Publishers, Inc.
40 Industrial Road
Box 398
Berkeley Heights, NJ 07922
USA
http://www.enslow.com

Library of Congress Cataloging-in-Publication Data

Smith, Linda Wasmer.
Louis Pasteur : genius disease fighter / Linda Wasmer Smith.
pages cm. — (Genius scientists and their genius ideas)
Includes bibliographical references and index.
Audience: Grades 4-6.
ISBN 978-0-7660-6575-8
1. Pasteur, Louis, 1822–1895—Juvenile literature. 2. Milk—Pasteurization—History—Juvenile literature. 3. Rabies vaccines—History—Juvenile literature. 4. Scientists—France—Biography—Juvenile literature. 5. Microbiologists—France—Biography—Juvenile literature. I. Title.
Q143.P2S55 2015
579.092—dc23
[B] 2014031254

Future Editions:
Paperback ISBN: 978-0-7660-6576-5
EPUB ISBN: 978-0-7660-6577-2
Single-User PDF ISBN: 978-0-7660-6578-9
Multi-User PDF: 978-0-7660-6579-6

Printed in the United States of America

102014 Bang Printing, Brainerd, Minn.

10 9 8 7 6 5 4 3 2 1

To Our Readers: We have done our best to make sure all Internet Addresses in this book were active and appropriate when we went to press. However, the author and the publisher have no control over and assume no liability for the material available on those Internet sites or on other Web sites they may link to. Any comments or suggestions can be sent by e-mail to comments@enslow.com or to the address on the back cover.

Enslow Publishers, Inc., is committed to printing our books on recycled paper. The paper in every book contains 10% to 30% post-consumer waste (PCW). The cover board on the outside of each book contains 100% PCW. Our goal is to do our part to help young people and the environment too!

Illustration Credits: ©Clipart.com, p. 22; From the book *A Life of Pasteur*, Hachette, 1922: Lebayle drawing depicting Louis Pasteur in 1845 at the École Normale Supérieure, from a daguerreotype, p. 8; National Library of Medicine, pp. 17, 45, 66; Wikipedia.com Public Domain Image, Created by Carmel830, p. 35; The French Government Tourist Office, p. 13; ©Thinkstock: (Baloncici/iStock, p. 39; Tuayai/iStock, p. 50; Photos.com, pp. 1, 57, 73).

Cover Illustration: ©Thinkstock: decade3d/iStock (Rabies Cell in Fluid); Shutterstock.com: ©Marish (light bulb icon)

Chapter 1

A Hero Is Born

The Christmas of 1822 must have been a joyous one for the Pasteur family. A new baby was on the way. The Pasteurs' first child, a son, had died while still a baby. Their second child, a daughter named Virginie, had been born in 1818. Now a third child was due any day.

The Pasteur family lived in Dôle, a small town in eastern France. The father, Jean-Joseph Pasteur, was a tanner—a person who makes animal hides into leather. Jean-Joseph's own father had also been a tanner. You might think that he would want his child to grow up to be a tanner, too, but Jean-Joseph had bigger dreams.

As a young man, Jean-Joseph had seen something of the wider world. He had fought as a soldier in the army of Napoleon I, the emperor of France and one of the greatest military geniuses of his time. Napoleon built an empire that covered most of western and central Europe. That empire collapsed in 1814. But Jean-Joseph never forgot those days of glory, when France seemed to rule the world.[1]

From that time on, Jean-Joseph spent many nights reading books. He tried to teach himself about history and science, and he hoped one day to have a son who would become a teacher in the local school.[2]

In 1816, Jean-Joseph had married Jeanne Roqui, the daughter of a gardener. Jeanne was a lively woman, a good match for her quiet husband. The couple lived in the same small building that held Jean-Joseph's tannery, and Jeanne worked hard to make this humble home a happy one.

On December 27, 1822, the Pasteurs' third child was born. The baby was a boy, and they named him Louis. Here at last was the son they had wanted so much. Louis would, in fact, grow up to be a professor. He would also become one of the greatest scientists of his day and a founder of modern medicine.

Pasteur the Scientist

Louis Pasteur's discoveries about how germs spread disease would help save countless lives. Germs—also called microbes—are tiny living things that can cause disease. Although too small to be seen without a microscope, germs have a powerful impact.

Pasteur would also make his mark as the inventor of pasteurization. This is a process for heating milk or other liquids hot enough and long enough to kill harmful microbes called bacteria.

In addition, Pasteur would go on to develop the rabies vaccine. Rabies is a deadly disease of the nervous system produced by a virus—a disease-causing agent even smaller than bacteria. People can get rabies from the bite of an infected animal, such as a dog, cat, raccoon, bat, or fox. A vaccine is a preparation of weakened or killed microbes that is given to people to prevent a disease. Until rabies could be prevented this way, people always died when they got the disease from an infected animal. Even more important, this early vaccine helped lay the groundwork for immunology, the branch of science that studies the body's natural defenses against disease.

Pasteur the Man

Of course, there were other great scientists who lived at the same time as Pasteur. Few, however, were as honored as he was then. That's because Pasteur was thought of not only as a genius, but also as a hero. It was said that he devoted his own life to making life better for all people. In fact, the English surgeon Stephen Paget (1855–1926) once called Pasteur "the most perfect man who has ever entered the Kingdom of Science."[3]

Louis Pasteur was without a doubt a remarkable man, but he was not perfect. Like anyone else, he had his flaws. One may have been a lack of total honesty. When Pasteur was fifty-five, he told his family never to show anyone his private lab notebooks. For many years, they did as he

Louis Pasteur at age eighteen

wished. Only when Pasteur's grandson died in 1971, did scientists have a chance to see what Louis Pasteur had written in the notebooks.

These notebooks were records of Pasteur's experiments. It turns out that he did not always do his experiments exactly the way he claimed. In a few cases, he may have altered his results to make his work look better.[4]

Yet these notebooks show the best side of Pasteur, too. Page after page, the 102 notebooks record a lifetime of hard, careful work. For forty years, Pasteur and his helpers spent almost every day on his research. There are perhaps ten thousand pages in all that are filled with Pasteur's hard-to-read handwriting.

Pasteur made not just one, but several big discoveries in his career. This led some people to say that he was lucky. Pasteur himself said that "chance favors only the prepared mind."[5] In other words, luck only helps those who are ready to recognize it. Pasteur's greatest gift may have been his ability to notice the little things that other people missed. Some of those little things proved to be the source of his lucky breaks.

2 Chapter

Life at the Tannery

Louis Pasteur and his family moved two times before he was five years old. In 1825, they moved to the nearby town of Marnoz, his mother's native village. Then they moved to the neighboring town of Arbois in 1827.

Arbois sits at the foot of the Jura Mountains in eastern France. The town is surrounded by lovely meadows and vineyards, fields planted with grapevines. Louis's family soon came to love the place. This is where Louis grew up. And even after he was famous, this is where he spent his summers.

By the time the Pasteurs settled in Arbois, there were two more members of the family. In addition to his older sister, Virginie, Louis had two younger sisters. Josephine was born while the family lived in Dôle, and Emilie was born in Marnoz.

The four Pasteur children and their parents shared a small house in Arbois. They lived above the tanning tubs there. This house is now a museum. Visitors can see Louis's school prizes and science books, among other items there.

Developing an Artist's Eye

In 1829, Louis began school in Arbois. As a young boy, he was just an average student. He showed no early signs of scientific genius. It was not until he was a teenager that Louis started winning many prizes for his schoolwork.

In fact, Louis's main talent as a boy seemed to be as an artist. Many of his pastel drawings of friends and family have been saved. They show that young Louis had a good eye for detail. In one portrait of his mother, she wears a white bonnet and a blue-and-green-checked shawl. Her face has a pleasant but determined look. This seems to be what Louis's mother was really like, both in looks and in character.[1]

One interesting fact about Louis's drawings is that the people he drew are never smiling. They are always solemn and formal. This is not unlike Louis himself. Even as a child, Louis was serious and dutiful. And as an adult, he usually looked as serious as he probably felt. Only one picture is known to show Louis smiling.[2]

When Louis was eight, something happened that stuck in his mind for the rest of his life. A wolf with rabies wandered out of the woods of the Jura Mountains. It attacked and bit several people around Arbois. At the time, such bites were usually treated by burning them with a red-hot iron. No one was sure why burning the bites seemed to stop some people from getting rabies. But the treatment did not always work. Some people who had their bites burned this way still became sick from rabies and died.

Many of the wolf's victims came to the village blacksmith to have their wounds burned. The blacksmith shop in Arbois was located near the Pasteur home. Louis watched the scene in horror. From where he stood, he could hear the victims' screams of pain. Louis remembered this experience as an adult. It may be one reason he was later driven to try to find a way to prevent rabies.[3]

Blossoming as a Student

As Louis grew up, he became a better student. When he was fifteen, he won a number of prizes at his school in Arbois. The headmaster urged him to prepare to take the entrance exam for the École Normale Supérieure in Paris. This was a college that trained people to become professors of the sciences or arts. Only a handful of students with top exam scores were admitted to the École Normale.

Louis's father decided to send him away to boarding school. This was difficult for the tanner to afford, but he thought that his son would get the preparation he needed at the school. So, in October 1838, Louis and his friend Jules Vercel traveled to Paris. Louis was to attend a boarding school in Paris run by a man named Barbet.

The lab at the Pasteur home in Arbois, where Louis Pasteur worked during summer visits as an adult.

Louis and Jules set off on their long journey in a stage-coach. It was a wet and dreary morning when they left. As the church steeple of Arbois faded from view, Louis felt his heart sink. Nothing had prepared him for life in Paris, one of the world's busiest cities. As a village boy, he was simply not ready for the crowded buildings and noisy streets. Soon Louis was feeling deeply homesick.[4]

Barbet was so worried by Louis's sadness that he wrote to Louis's parents. In November 1838, Louis's father brought him home to Arbois. How did Louis feel about his failure to adjust to Paris? He may have been a bit ashamed, but that just made him work all the harder. Back at school in Arbois, he once again excelled. In fact, he won so many prizes at year's end that he could not carry them all. It seems that Louis was still determined to make a success of his life.

Chapter 3

The Call of Science

Louis Pasteur had not given up his dream of studying at the École Normale. He decided to try preparatory school again. In 1839, he began attending the Royal College of Besançon. The town of Besançon is only about twenty-five miles from Arbois. Louis's father went there every month to sell leather goods from his tannery.

Perhaps the regular visits from his father helped, for this time Pasteur overcame his homesickness. He did quite well in his classes at the college. In addition, he still liked to draw and paint. After one of his portraits was shown in the parlor of the college, he became known around town as "the artist."[1]

Pasteur enjoyed the praise he received for his artwork. Yet he knew it would not get him into the École Normale.[2] So he began to aim his attention in a new direction. In

1840, he took the exam for his Bachelor of Letters degree. He passed with "fair" marks in history and geography and "good" marks in Greek, Latin, language, and philosophy. But his only "excellent" mark came in basic science.

Setting his Sights on Science

Pasteur was now determined to study science at the École Normale. But to do that, he first had to have a Bachelor of Science degree. To prepare for this second degree, he decided to stay at the Royal College of Besançon.

In his second year at the college, he was offered work as an assistant teacher. In return, he was given a room, meals, and a small salary. Although he was only eighteen, he was very busy as both a teacher and a student.

Pasteur passed the exam for his Bachelor of Science degree in 1842. Just days later, he passed the entrance exam for the École Normale.

Then something unexpected happened: Pasteur turned down the École Normale's offer of admission. He had ranked fifteenth on the entrance exam, but he felt that he could do better than that. So he decided to spend another year preparing. Even as a young man, Pasteur always strove for perfection.

Paris was the center of learning in France. Pasteur knew that he had to return there. So at age nineteen, he headed back to Barbet's boarding school. This time, though, Pasteur was ready for the city. He helped teach the younger students, and he took classes at the Lycée Saint-Louis, a leading preparatory school.

Pasteur as he appeared in most photographs—with a serious expression.

At year's end, Pasteur received first prize in physics, the branch of science that deals with matter and energy. When he took the École Normale exam again, he ranked fourth. It was finally time for Pasteur to fulfill his dream.

Studying at the École Normale

In October 1843, Pasteur entered the École Normale. There he would study physics and chemistry, the science of substances and chemical elements and the changes and their reactions. One day, he would be a professor there.

École Normale students spent many hours in classes. In addition, they spent an hour every day using what they had learned. They might blow glass, build machines or make locks and keys. Pasteur worked hard at his lessons, so hard that his father worried about his health. But Pasteur was happy that he was on the road to a career that would bring good pay and much respect. He had also started on the way to making his mark in science.[3]

A high point of Pasteur's student days in Paris was going to the lectures of Jean-Baptiste Dumas. This man was one of the greatest chemists of his day. He was also a powerful speaker, and Pasteur was deeply impressed.[4] Dressed in formal-looking black, Dumas delivered his lectures to large audiences. His talks were clear and interesting, and his demonstrations were flawless.

Jean-Baptiste Dumas sparked Pasteur's desire to learn more about chemistry. Now his favorite way to pass free time was working in the lab or taking a private lesson from Dumas's assistant.

Pasteur had one more exam to take before becoming a professor. A good result on this qualifying exam would open doors to the best jobs. Pasteur took the exam in 1846 and placed third in physical science. The professors who gave the test were impressed by his efforts. "He will make an excellent professor," they wrote.[5]

Heeding the Call of Chemistry

Pasteur was already heading down an important path. A month after the qualifying exam, he was offered a job as an assistant in chemistry. He would help the famous chemist Antoine-Jérôme Balard.

Twenty years earlier, Balard discovered the chemical element called bromine. In later years, though, he was known not only for that accomplishment, but also for his simple living habits. It was said that when Balard traveled, he took with him only a shirt and socks, wrapped in newspaper and carried in a pocket.

Not surprisingly, Balard's lab was simple, too. He even liked to make his students build their own equipment. Yet there Pasteur could do the research that would lead to a more advanced Doctor of Science degree. It was also in this lab that Pasteur made the first of many important discoveries.

4 Chapter

Gazing at Crystals

Louis Pasteur was ready to begin his own research. He chose to study crystals, the regularly shaped objects that many substances form when they harden. Crystals have both sharp edges and flat surfaces. Snow is nothing more than water vapor that has frozen into crystals. Now imagine the lacy shape of a snowflake. It is easy to see why the artist in Pasteur would be drawn to the beauty of crystals. But Pasteur also was determined to solve the mystery behind crystals.

Ordinary light from the sun or a lamp is made up of waves that vibrate, or shake back and forth, in all directions. Polarized light, on the other hand, is made up of orderly waves that vibrate in only one direction. It was already known that some crystals rotate, or turn, the direction in which polarized light vibrates. This property is called optical activity.

It was also known that some crystals turn light to the right, while others turn it to the left. This seemed to be related to the shape of the crystal. Some crystals were shaped in a "right-handed" way and rotated light to the right, while others were "left-handed" and rotated light to the left.

Making the First Big Discovery

Pasteur focused on two kinds of crystals that formed in the vats where wine was made. They are called tartaric acid and racemic acid. There was something strange about these crystals: while they seemed to have the same shape, the tartaric acid was optically active, but the racemic acid was not.

Pasteur thought there had to be something different about the two types of crystals. He was sure that this difference had never been noticed before, and he was determined to find out what it was.

Pasteur began his work with crystals in 1847. He completed his Doctor of Science degree in August of that year, but his interest in crystals continued. Pasteur spent many hours hunched over his lab bench. He peered tirelessly through a microscope at the crystals, and he used his artist's skill to draw what he saw there. He also built special instruments for measuring the way the crystals rotated light.

Then something exciting happened. One day in April 1848, Pasteur looked up from his lab bench and exclaimed, "I have it!"[1] What he had found were tiny surfaces called

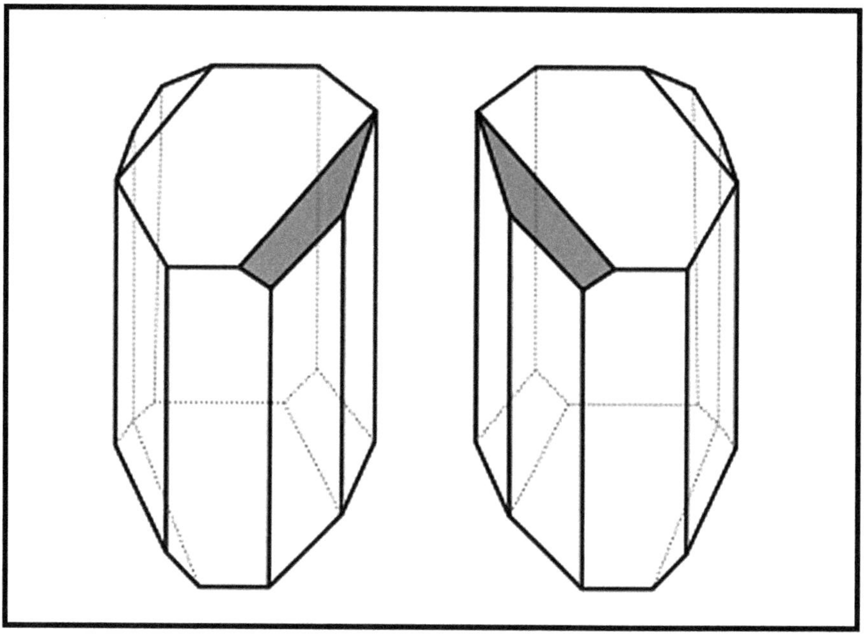

Dextro (right-hand) and levorotary (left-hand) forms of tartrate. Pasteur separated the left and right crystal shapes from each other to form two piles of crystals: In solution one form rotated light to the left, the other to the right, while an equal mixture of the two forms canceled each other's effect, and did not rotate the polarized light.

facets. All the facets in tartaric acid pointed in the same direction. But in racemic acid, some facets pointed one way, while others pointed in the opposite direction. No one had noticed these facets before.

Pasteur hypothesized that some of the racemic acid facets rotated light to the right and others to the left. The two kinds of facets combined canceled each other out, which explained why racemic acid was not optically active. When Pasteur tested this idea in the lab, the results were just as he had predicted.

Pasteur was so thrilled by his findings that he rushed from the lab. He grabbed a lab assistant and said, "I have just made a great discovery."[2] Then he led the man outside into the garden and told him about what he had found.

Pasteur was only twenty-five years old at the time. News of the young man's remarkable discovery soon spread throughout Paris. It reached French scientist Jean-Baptiste Biot, who had earlier done important work on optical activity. Biot had Pasteur repeat the experiment for him. When he saw the results, Biot exclaimed, "My dear son, I have loved science so deeply that this stirs my heart."[3]

A New Branch of Chemistry

While studying crystals, Pasteur had been fascinated by the fact that some crystals came in "right-handed" and "left-handed" shapes. If you look at your own right and left hands, you'll see that they are similar but not quite the same. Like your hands, the mirror images of these crystal shapes did not match up perfectly. It was impossible to rotate one shape so that it lined up exactly with the other. Pasteur realized that this difference must be important.

The realization was Pasteur's first big contribution to science. His work formed the basis of stereochemistry, a new branch of chemistry. Stereochemistry deals with the position in space of tiny particles called atoms and how this position affects such things as optical activity. Today it is still a very important area of research.

Pasteur believed this line of research would one day shed light on the chemistry of life itself. It turns out he was right. Take enzymes, for example. Enzymes are substances that speed up chemical reactions inside living things. Without enzymes, these reactions would occur too slowly or not at all, and life would not be possible. We now know that enzymes often recognize only the right-handed or left-handed form of a compound.

Moving to Strasbourg

Around this same time, there was much excitement outside the walls of the École Normale. The French king was unpopular. A revolution had broken out, and Paris was in an uproar. Pasteur even joined the National Guard, a citizen army. Then in May 1848, his mother died. Pasteur blamed her death partly on her worries about his safety. He decided that it would be best if he left Paris.

That fall, Pasteur moved to the French city of Dijon. He worked as a physics professor at a local school there, but he hoped to get a better teaching job soon.[4] That wish would come true within a matter of weeks.

In January 1849, Pasteur became a professor of chemistry at the University of Strasbourg, located in northeastern France. Pasteur continued his studies on crystals at the university in addition to teaching. During his five years at Strasbourg, Pasteur received the first major honors of his career. In 1853, for example, he was given the Legion of Honor medal.

Marrying and Starting a Family

The most important change in Pasteur's life at this time had nothing to do with work. Soon after arriving in Strasbourg, Pasteur met the daughter of a university official. Her name was Marie Laurent.

Marie was twenty-two years old at the time. She was a gentle young woman with clear blue eyes. For Pasteur, it was love at first sight. The custom of the day was to ask a woman's parents for permission to marry her. In February 1849, Pasteur penned a frank letter to Marie's father. He wrote, "My only assets are good health, an honest heart, and my position at the university."[5]

Marie's father must have felt that was quite enough. Louis Pasteur and Marie Laurent were married in Strasbourg on May 29, 1849. According to legend, Pasteur spent the morning of his wedding day working in his lab. He became so wrapped up in what he was doing there that he had to be reminded to go to the church.[6]

Louis and Marie Pasteur's marriage lasted forty-six years, until Pasteur's death in 1895. By all accounts, it was a splendid match. Marie Pasteur understood her husband's devotion to science. She helped with his work and accepted the long hours.

Their first three children were born while the Pasteurs still lived in Strasbourg. Their oldest child, a daughter named Jeanne, was born in 1850. Their son, Jean-Baptiste, was born the following year. He was named after Jean-Baptiste Biot. Another daughter, Cécile, arrived in 1853. Two more daughters followed in later years: Marie-Louise, born in 1858, and Camille, born in 1863.

The Strasbourg years were an exciting time for the Pasteur family. They also marked the start of Pasteur's long and fruitful career. Pasteur himself seemed to sense this. He wrote to a friend that his wife sometimes scolded him for working so hard. "I console her," he wrote, "by telling her that I will lead her to posterity."[7]

Chapter 5

THE BEET JUICE PROBLEM

The year 1854 found Pasteur ready for another change. He took a new job as professor of chemistry and dean of sciences at the University of Lille. The city of Lille, in northern France, is a center of industry. It was understood that Pasteur would focus his teaching and research on the practical needs of the region.

Then, as now, some scientists felt that they should care only about pure science. They were concerned strictly with theories that explain the world using observations and reasoning. However, Pasteur also believed in the value of applied science. He thought it was part of a scientist's job to put ideas to practical use.

One day in 1856, a man named Bigo asked Pasteur for help. Bigo owned a local factory where alcohol was made, in this case from beet juice. Alcohol is a colorless liquid that is sometimes used in manufacturing and medicine.

The production of alcohol was a major industry in Lille. Bigo was having problems producing pure alcohol. He turned to Pasteur, who was his son's professor, for advice.

Fermenting New Ideas

Alcohol is produced from beet juice by a process known as fermentation. This is a gradual chemical change in which sugar is changed into alcohol and carbon dioxide gas. Sugar is found in foods such as beets. It is also found in grapes, which naturally turn into wine as a result of fermentation. Thus, fermentation is the source of the alcohol found in alcoholic beverages.

Pasteur became a frequent visitor to Bigo's factory. He took some of the fermenting juice back to his lab. He looked at the juice using a microscope. Then he wrote descriptions and made drawings of what he saw. This was one of the things that prompted Pasteur to study fermentation. He grew fascinated with the subject. It became the center of his research for several years.

At the time, people already knew that yeast had a role in fermentation. We now know that yeast is made up of tiny, one-celled living things that grow quickly in the presence of sugar. You may be familiar with a common use for the yeast you can buy in the supermarket: it makes bread dough rise. The carbon dioxide bubbles produced during fermentation are what cause the dough to swell.

Back in the 1830s, the German scientist Theodor Schwann declared that fermentation was due to living yeast cells. Most scientists at that time still thought that fermentation was a purely chemical process. As a chemist, Pasteur might have been expected to share this strictly chemical view. But his careful observations with the microscope had convinced him that fermentation was rooted in life. He set out to prove this.

In August 1857, Pasteur presented a famous paper. It dealt with lactic acid fermentation. This is the kind of fermentation that occurs when lactose, the sugar in milk, is changed into lactic acid. That is what happens when milk turns sour.

Germ Theory of Fermentation

Pasteur's paper laid out two revolutionary ideas on fermentation. First, it said that microorganisms cause fermentation. Microorganisms are living things too small to be seen without a microscope. Yeast and bacteria are examples of microorganisms. Second, it said that specific kinds of microorganisms cause specific types of fermentation. For example, yeast is the microorganism that produces alcoholic fermentation. Another kind of microorganism would produce a different kind of change.

What Pasteur had seen in Bigo's beet juice now made sense. Some of the tiny shapes he had viewed under the microscope were living yeast cells, needed to change sugar into alcohol. However, other tiny shapes he had seen there were different microorganisms that were causing the unwanted changes. They were the reason Bigo was having trouble making good alcohol.

Pasteur's 1857 paper is still considered a landmark in science. It introduced what is called the germ theory of fermentation. Later he would help develop the even more important germ theory of disease. Today Pasteur is known as a founder of microbiology, the branch of science that deals with microorganisms.

Teaching at the École Normale

Once again, a major discovery meant a major change for Pasteur. In October 1857, he became director of scientific studies at the École Normale, his old school. This was an important job, but it did not provide a lab. So Pasteur's first task upon returning to Paris was to find a place to carry out his research.

Pasteur soon found two unused rooms in an attic. The roof was so low there that he was unable to stand up straight. Yet Pasteur set about turning these rooms into a lab. A couple of years later, he moved his lab into a building with five small rooms on two floors. Even there, space was quite limited. In fact, he kept some of his equipment under a staircase. The only way to reach it was by crawling.

Pasteur was also short on money. In 1859, he wrote to France's Minister of Public Education: "I have absolutely no means to meet the everyday expenses of my research work."[1] Money was a worry for many years to come. Yet despite these problems, Pasteur made great progress.

Then tragedy struck the Pasteur family. The Pasteurs' oldest child, Jeanne, visited her grandfather in Arbois.

There she became ill with typhoid fever, a disease that causes a high fever and attacks the intestines. Jeanne died in September 1859. Her father was heartbroken by her death.

Nothing could keep Pasteur from his work for long, however. The very next year marked the start of a new direction in his research. It was a crucial turning point not only in Pasteur's life, but also in the history of science.

6 Chapter

The Swan-Necked Flask

In 1860, a debate raged in scientific circles in Paris. People were talking about a book published the year before by Félix-Archimède Pouchet. The book dealt with spontaneous generation, the theory that living things can arise from nonliving matter. Pouchet claimed that the theory was correct.

Many people disagreed, but this side needed a strong voice. The Academy of Sciences offered a cash prize to the scientist who could produce the best proof for or against spontaneous generation.

Pasteur wanted to see the issue settled once and for all.[1] He also needed the money. So he entered the debate, despite being new to biology, the science that deals with living things. A series of clever experiments followed. By the time Pasteur was finished, he had won the 2,500-franc prize. More important, he had shown beyond doubt that the theory of spontaneous generation was false.

Disproving Spontaneous Generation

In a famous set of experiments, Pasteur put liquid into several flasks, or glass bottles. Then he boiled the liquid, driving the air out of the flasks, which killed or pushed out microorganisms that were already there. Finally he sealed the flasks to keep microorganisms from getting back in. Pasteur took the flasks to different spots, where he opened them briefly. He let the outside air, which carried new microorganisms, make contact with the liquid inside. Then he resealed the flasks and took them back to his lab for observation.

Pasteur waited and watched to see what would grow in the formerly pure liquid. This would show which microorganisms were in the surrounding air. He found that when the flasks were opened in dusty streets and cellars, the liquid was soon cloudy with microorganisms. But he still needed to show that it was microorganisms in the air, and not just air itself, that gave rise to this life.

Pasteur hypothesized that the cleaner the air, the fewer the microorganisms it would contain. To test this, he went to his childhood home of Arbois. He opened twenty flasks in the countryside there. Then he strapped another twenty flasks on a mule's back and climbed to an icy mountain peak. There he opened the flasks to the cold, fresh wind. Microorganisms later grew in eight of the samples from the country, but they grew in only one of the samples from the mountain with its nearly germ-free air.

Pasteur used swan-necked flasks for some of his experiments. The glass necks of these flasks were shaped like a long "S." They did indeed look like the graceful necks of swans. Pasteur's old chemistry professor, Antoine-Jérôme Balard, had suggested this shape. Even though the flasks were left unsealed, no microorganisms grew inside.

Air was getting into the open flasks. However, Pasteur argued that microorganisms in the air were becoming trapped in the bend of the flask necks. That was why the liquid stayed pure. To prove his point, Pasteur tilted the flasks so that the liquid poured into the neck bends. Microorganisms soon appeared.

The debate over spontaneous generation came to a head in 1864. On April 7, Pasteur gave a lecture on the subject at the Sorbonne, a college at the University of Paris. Scientists, writers, and even a princess came to hear him speak. They were expecting a great performance, and Pasteur did not disappoint. He showed the audience one of his swan-necked flasks. He told them, "Never will the doctrine of spontaneous generation recover from the mortal blow of this simple experiment."[2]

Discovering Anaerobic Bacteria

At the same time, Pasteur was also working on other problems. One day, he was looking through a microscope at a drop of sugary liquid that was fermenting. At first, all the bacteria in the drop were very active. But soon Pasteur

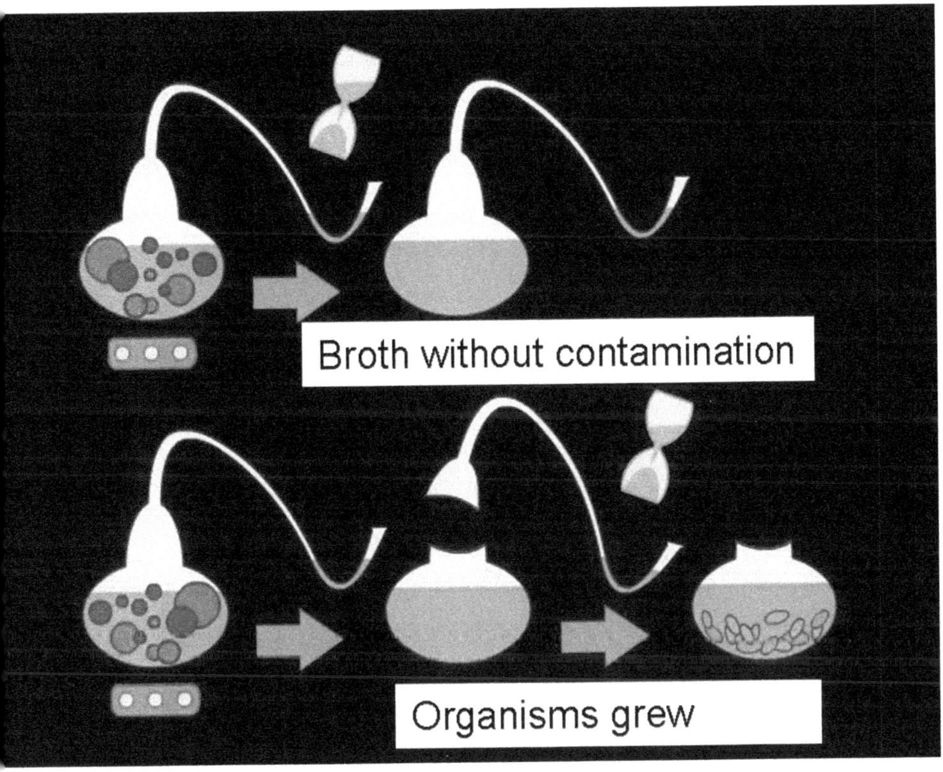

(Top) A swan-necked flask with broth and no bacteria in it after being boiled to remove any germs or microorganisms.

(Below) Another swan-necked flask with outside contaminants in the air allowed in. This broth grows microorganisms.

noticed something odd: the bacteria around the edge of the drop had stopped moving, while those in the center of the drop still moved.

Pasteur guessed that air—or more precisely, the oxygen in air—was bad for these bacteria. It turned out to be a good guess. Pasteur was the first scientist to realize that some bacteria are only active when no oxygen is present. He called these bacteria "anaerobic," from the Greek for "without air."

Pasteur was very busy throughout this time. In addition to his work at the École Normale, he began teaching science at the École des Beaux-Arts in Paris. This was a school of fine arts. Among other things, he taught about the chemistry of paints.

Pasteur had made a name for himself as a brilliant scientist. Word of his accomplishments had even reached Emperor Napoleon III, the nephew of Napoleon. The emperor asked to meet with Pasteur at the royal palace in Paris.

What a thrill this must have been for the scientist! He had been raised on stories of French glory. Now he was talking to the emperor himself. During their meeting, the emperor asked Pasteur to study the problems of winemaking. Pasteur agreed, and he never forgot his promise.

Chapter 7

From Grapes to Wine

In Pasteur's day, as now, France was famous for its wines. Since Pasteur had grown up near vineyards, he was well aware of this fact. He had not forgotten his goal of helping French industries. So perhaps it was natural that he would one day turn his knowledge of fermentation to helping the winemakers.

Wine is made from fermented grapes. The process, however, is as much an art as a science. Sometimes everything would go just right, and the taste would be perfect. Other times, something would go wrong. The wine would end up bitter or sour. Pasteur hoped to find out how to prevent such problems.

Helping the Winemakers

Pasteur remembered what he had seen in the beet juice from Bigo's factory. Other microorganisms besides yeast were present when the alcohol went bad. He guessed that this was also true when the wine soured.

In addition, Pasteur knew that vinegar was made from alcohol created by fermentation. Vinegar has a very sour taste. Pasteur thought the same bacterium (a single type of bacteria) that produces vinegar might be making the wine go bad.

To test his theory, Pasteur turned to his childhood friends in Arbois. He set up a makeshift lab for the study of wine in an old café there. Since the café sign was left in the window, people sometimes came by looking for food. They usually stopped at the door when they saw the strange-looking equipment inside.

Pasteur studied many samples of wine under his microscope. He found that his theory was correct. There were a number of problems that could affect a wine's taste. And most problems could be traced to a particular microorganism. For example, *Mycoderma aceti* is the bacterium that is involved in the production of vinegar. As Pasteur had suspected, this bacterium can also make wine go sour.

Inventing the Pasteurization Process

The next step was to rid the wine of these unwanted microorganisms. In 1865, Pasteur began treating wine with heat. He found that he could kill off harmful bacteria by heating wine for several minutes to 55°C (131°F). The process did not change the wine's taste, and wine treated this way could be stored indefinitely.

A modern milk processing plant, where raw milk is heated (pasteurized) in order to kill harmful bacteria.

Sterilization is the act of getting rid of microorganisms. The process of heating a liquid just hot enough and long enough to kill harmful bacteria is called partial sterilization. However, this process soon became better known by another name: pasteurization, in honor of its inventor.

It was soon shown that pasteurization could be used for many kinds of drinks and foods. These include juices, eggs, spices, and ice cream. Nearly all of the milk sold in the United States today is pasteurized. Typically, milk is heated to 63° C (145° F) for at least thirty minutes, or to 72° C (161° F) for fifteen seconds. Pasteurization lets the milk stay fresh longer before going sour. It also prevents some diseases that are caused by bacteria found in untreated milk.

Today, two other types of milk pasteurization are sometimes used as well. Ultrapasteurization involves heating milk to at least 138° C (280° F) for at least two seconds. As long as the container stays unopened, ultrapasteurized milk can be kept in the refrigerator for 60 to 90 days. Ultra-high-temperature (UHT) pasteurization involves heating milk between 138° and 150° C (280°–302° F) for one or two seconds. The milk is then packaged in germ-free, airtight containers. An unopened container of UHT milk can be stored for up to 90 days without refrigeration.[1]

"Pasteurization" is now a familiar word around the world. It is one way Pasteur's name lives on more than a century after his death.

Chapter 8

SAVING THE SILKWORMS

Wine-making was not the only industry that needed Pasteur's help. In the mid-1800s, French silkmakers also faced a crisis. Silk is a kind of fine, soft cloth made from threads spun by silkworms. A mysterious disease was killing off the silkworms. The lack of silk posed a major problem for the French clothing industry.

The chemist Jean-Baptiste Dumas came from the part of France where silk was produced. He asked Pasteur to head a group studying the silkworm problem. At the time, Pasteur knew nothing of silkworms or their diseases. When he pointed this out, Dumas replied, "So much the better! For ideas, you will have only those which shall come to you as a result of your own observations."[1] Louis Pasteur accepted the challenge.

Studying Silkworm Diseases

In June 1865, at age forty-two, Pasteur traveled from Paris to Alais. This town (now called Alés) in southern France was in the heart of the silk-making region. Pasteur set up a research lab there. He returned to Alais every summer through 1869.

Pasteur quickly learned that one disease affecting the silkworms caused small black spots on their skin. Since these spots looked like grains of pepper, the disease was called *pébrine*—from *pébré,* French slang for pepper.

Just nine days after Pasteur's arrival in Alais, however, he was called away. His father was very ill. By the time Pasteur reached Arbois, his father was already dead. The loss touched Pasteur deeply. He wrote: "Dear Marie, dear children, the dear grandfather is no more; we have taken him this morning to his last resting place, close to little Jeanne's."[2] Yet Pasteur also wrote that he must go back to Alais. His study of silkworms would be seriously set back if he did not return soon to his lab.

Once in Alais, Pasteur began studying both sick and healthy silkworms. When he looked at the sick silkworms under a microscope, he saw oval shapes. Pasteur did not grasp the importance of these oval shapes at first. Finally he guessed that the silkworms were infected with some microbe. Proving this, however, took much hard work and many false starts.

Silkworms are actually the larva, or caterpillar, stage of a moth. This moth lays its eggs in early summer. The tiny silkworms hatch from the eggs. They eat constantly until they are fully grown. Then they spin silky cases called cocoons around themselves. Silk is made from the threads in these cocoons. While inside the cocoon, the silkworm changes into a pupa. After it emerges from the cocoon, the pupa changes into an adult moth, which mates and lays eggs. Then the whole life cycle begins again.

Pasteur showed that *pébrine* could be controlled by a process known as the egg-selection method. Some of the moths were checked under a microscope for signs of disease. If such signs were found, the moths and any eggs they had laid were destroyed. In this way, only healthy silkworms would be allowed to hatch.

Some people complained that a microscope was fine for scientists, but silkworm growers would never be able to use one. Pasteur responded: "There is in my laboratory a little girl eight years of age who had learned to use it without difficulty."[3] This little girl was his daughter Marie-Louise, who often helped out in his lab.

During 1866, Pasteur used the egg-selection method to pick batches of eggs that should have been healthy. As he expected, most of the silkworms that hatched from these eggs were free of disease. But some were not. These silkworms did not have the skin spots seen in *pébrine.* Instead, they had soft, flabby bodies.

Pasteur finally showed that *pébrine* was not the only disease killing the silkworms. At least one other disease was attacking the silkworms as well. Often both diseases infected the same silkworm, which just made things more confusing. Pasteur worked out a method for controlling the spread of this second disease as well.

In 1867, Pasteur came up with a bold way to show the usefulness of his methods. He sent a trade journal batches of silkworm eggs along with his predictions of which would be healthy. These predictions were sealed, to be opened only after the silkworms had hatched. Pasteur's predictions turned out to be correct.

Tragedies, One After Another

Pasteur's successes were all the more remarkable because they came at a time of great sadness. Louis and Marie Pasteur's youngest child, Camille, died in September 1865, just months after the death of Pasteur's father. Camille was only two years old at the time. Then, in May 1866, while working in Alais, Pasteur received word that his daughter Cécile was gravely ill with typhoid fever. She died days later.

Such losses were all too common in the years before vaccines and antibiotic drugs—medicines that work against diseases caused by bacteria and certain other microorganisms. Diseases such as typhoid fever, diphtheria, pertussis (also called whooping cough), and scarlet fever were frequent killers of children. Yet the death of a child was every bit as painful as it is today. Pasteur was deeply affected. In a letter to his wife, he mourned, "Our beloved children die one after another!"[4]

Still, Pasteur continued to work long hours at Alais. In addition to his lab there, he set up a silkworm farm for

Louis Pasteur dictates a paper to his wife, Marie, at Alais. While at Alais, Pasteur would remedy an epidemic that was causing the death of silkworms, and thus hurting the French economy.

testing his ideas. There was always much to do. There were silkworms to be raised and eggs to be collected. There were countless experiments to be run. The mulberry leaves that the silkworms ate had to be harvested, and the mice that liked to eat the silkworms had to be controlled. In the evenings, Pasteur would dictate letters, journal articles, and book chapters to his busy wife.

Opening a New Chemistry Lab

Each fall, Pasteur returned to Paris, where he continued to teach students and do research at the École Normale. His duties there also included helping run the school itself. He oversaw such matters as the students' rooms and food, and he enforced the school's rules. Pasteur was very strict. This made him unpopular with many students.[5]

In 1867, Pasteur lost his old job at the École Normale after a student protest. The school officials in charge did not want to lose such a respected scientist, so they agreed when Pasteur proposed a new job for himself: director of an enlarged chemistry lab. They also agreed that Pasteur could teach chemistry at the Sorbonne.

The long hours and heavy duties must have taken a toll. One day in October 1868, Pasteur had been feeling unwell and extremely tired, but he still attended a meeting of the Academy of Sciences. Upon returning home, he went to bed early. That evening, the forty-five-year-old scientist suffered a stroke. This occurs when the blood supply to part of the brain is interrupted or severely reduced, depriving brain tissue of oxygen and food. The sudden loss of brain functioning can lead to a number of effects, including paralysis, which is the loss of voluntary movement in part of the body.

Just after the stroke, Pasteur was completely unable to speak or move the left side of his body. Slowly, much of his strength returned. But he never totally regained his ability to speak, walk, and work with his hands as before. From that time on, Pasteur needed the help of assistants to carry out some of his experiments. And Pasteur had a reputation for being as demanding of his assistants as he was of himself.

Not even a stroke could stop Pasteur's work for long. In 1869, he was invited to Villa Vicentina, an estate in Austria owned by a prince. Silkworms were grown there. Pasteur was asked to tackle the estate's *pébrine* problem.

Life at Villa Vicentina was more restful for Pasteur. He took walks and carriage rides. He even sometimes walked the ponies that were the delight of his two surviving children, Jean-Baptiste and Marie-Louise. In this peaceful setting, Pasteur finished writing a book on diseases of the silkworm. And the next summer, thanks to Pasteur's efforts, Villa Vicentina produced more silkworms than ever before.

9 Chapter

The Tiniest Enemies

Most people would not think that silkworms and humans had much in common. Pasteur came to believe that if microbes could cause diseases in silkworms, he reasoned, surely they could cause human diseases as well.

In the seventeenth century, the Dutch scientist Antoni van Leeuwenhoek had described "tiny animals" that he viewed with simple microscopes. Such microorganisms were still a mystery, though. People did not know that some could cause disease. In fact, one popular theory stated that disease was caused by poisonous fumes that were given off by decaying matter and blown about by the wind.

Pasteur's work with silkworms led him to the brink of some of his most important discoveries. Then history interfered. In 1870, France went to war against Prussia, a

German state. The war forced Pasteur to leave Paris and his work there. He took his family to Arbois until the war's end.

Louis and Marie Pasteur's son, Jean-Baptiste, was now a young man. He joined the French army to fight in the war. Pasteur waited anxiously for news of his son. The combination of worrying about his son and leaving his lab made this a difficult time in Pasteur's life.

Pasteur always loved his country dearly. He became so upset by the Prussian siege of the city of Paris that he returned an honorary doctoral degree given to him earlier by a German university. France's defeat in 1871 came as a blow to Pasteur.

Brewing the Beer of Revenge

After the war, Pasteur was offered a job as a chemistry professor at an Italian university. It would have meant more money for Pasteur, but he turned down the job. He refused to leave France in his country's time of need.

Instead, Pasteur vowed to help France in an unusual way. German beer was widely regarded as some of the best beer in the world. Pasteur decided to study beer, with the aim of making French beer even better than the German kind. He spoke of his project as "the beer of revenge."[1]

This idea came to Pasteur while he was visiting Émile Duclaux, a former student. Duclaux was then a professor in a French town with a nearby brewery, a place where beer is made. Pasteur saw this as a chance to expand his earlier work on fermentation. Soon he had shown that

Pasteur came to believe that if microbes could cause diseases in silkworms, surely they could cause human diseases as well.

unwanted changes in beer, like those in wine, were due to microorganisms. These changes could also be prevented with pasteurization.

Even after he returned to the École Normale in Paris, Pasteur kept studying beer. Eventually, Pasteur wrote a book on beer fermentation that greatly improved the brewing industry in France. Still bent on revenge, though, Pasteur refused to allow a German translation of his book. But, in the end, Pasteur's studies helped the French beer industry, although it was generally agreed that German beer was still better.

Pasteur's patriotism also showed up in another way around this time. In 1876, he decided to run for the Senate. He thought that if he were elected, he could help France regain its place as a center of learning. In his words: "If you honor me with your vote, I shall represent science in all its purity, dignity, and independence in the Senate."[2] Pasteur proved to be a poor candidate, though. He was badly defeated in the election.

Germ Theory of Disease

In 1877, Pasteur's interests took a new turn. He began focusing on the causes of disease. Twenty years before, Pasteur had first laid out his germ theory of fermentation. Later this set the stage for the even more important germ theory of disease. The theory stated that many diseases were caused by microbes. As with fermentation, each of this type of disease could be linked to a particular kind of microbe.

Pasteur was not the only scientist of his day working on such germ theories. His main rival was Robert Koch, a German doctor. Koch worked out a method for showing which type of bacteria causes a certain disease. Using the method, he was able to describe the complete life cycle of a particular kind of bacteria that causes anthrax. This is a disease that infects cattle, sheep, and goats, and can be spread to humans.

A great burst of progress followed. Between 1877 and 1888, Pasteur himself discovered the microbes that cause several animal and human diseases. In one case, he set about finding the source of a skin disease that bothered Émile Duclaux, his former student. Duclaux suffered from furunculosis, a skin disease that leads to painful, pus-filled swellings called boils. Pasteur traced Duclaux's problem to a particular type of Staphylococcus bacteria.

Pasteur was not willing to stop with just discoveries. As always, he wanted to put his findings to use solving practical problems. He suggested that certain diseases could be prevented by getting rid of the microbes that cause them.

One person who read about Pasteur's ideas was Joseph Lister, an English doctor. He grew convinced that microbes were causing the deaths of many patients who had surgery—an operation to treat disease or injury. Lister began covering surgical wounds with bandages that had been treated with a chemical compound called carbolic acid. This would kill any microbes around the wound. Lister also sprayed carbolic acid around the entire area where the surgery was done. As a result, fewer wounds became infected, and more surgical patients survived.

Lister is often considered the father of modern surgery. He was always quick to acknowledge his debt to Pasteur's writings. In an 1874 letter, Lister noted that his own ideas were based on Pasteur's germ theory. He invited Pasteur to visit his hospital, to see "how largely mankind is being benefited by your labours."[3]

Today doctors try to keep microbes away from surgical wounds in the first place instead of just trying to kill them. They wash their hands thoroughly before an operation, and they wear germ-free gloves and gowns. They also wear masks to help prevent the spread of microbes through the air. In addition, operating rooms are kept as clean as possible. Such measures have saved countless lives.

It is not surprising that Pasteur worried about microbes in his own life. Sometimes he took this concern a bit too far. He often refused to shake hands for fear of catching an illness. At the dinner table, he always wiped his glass and silverware in the hopes of getting rid of any dirt that might be there.

You might not go to such lengths. Yet you do know to cover your mouth when you cough to keep from spreading microbes through the air. And you know to wash your hands before cooking to keep from passing microbes on your skin. People did not always know how important microbes were, though. It was hard for them to believe something so tiny could be so powerful. Pasteur helped to change all that.

10 Chapter

Warfare Against Germs

Pasteur was not satisfied just to learn more about microbes. He wanted to fight back against them, too.[1] He dreamed that someday there would be a way to prevent infectious diseases. These are diseases that are caused by microbes and can be spread from one living thing to another. Many infectious diseases can be spread from human to human, or animal to human, or animal to animal.

In 1879, a disease called chicken cholera raged through the barnyards of France. Wherever it struck, it killed most of the chickens within a few days. Pasteur began to study the microbe that causes chicken cholera. First he cultured it—in other words, he grew it in the lab. He found that when healthy chickens were given a shot of the chicken cholera culture, they would die within a day or two.

Developing a Chicken Cholera Vaccine

That summer, Pasteur took a vacation, heading for Arbois. He left his cultures in the care of his lab assistants. One of these assistants was Émile Roux, who later became one of Pasteur's most important coworkers.

Legend has it that the lab assistants took a vacation, too. They left the cultures unattended for several weeks. It is also possible that Roux left the cultures alone on purpose to see what would happen. In any case, Pasteur returned from Arbois to find a lab full of old, dried-out cultures.

When chickens were injected with some of this old chicken cholera culture, they stayed healthy. It seemed the culture had lost its ability to cause disease. Then something surprising occurred. Both these chickens and some new ones were injected with fresh cultures. The new chickens soon died, but to everyone's amazement, most that had received the old culture too remained healthy.

The assistants were worried. What would Pasteur's reaction be? Pasteur was silent for a few minutes, as he thought about what had happened. Then he exclaimed, "Don't you see that these animals have been vaccinated!"[2]

A vaccinated animal or person is given a vaccine, a preparation of weakened or killed microbes that prevents a disease. At the time, only one type of vaccination was used. People in England had noticed that women employed by the dairies who got cowpox, a disease spread to humans by infected cows, later were less likely to get smallpox, a more serious disease that also caused a similar skin rash.

An English doctor named Edward Jenner set out to study this matter. In 1796, Jenner gave the first medical vaccination. He took the pus from a cowpox sore and put it into the arm of a healthy boy. As expected, the boy soon came down with cowpox. Later, Jenner gave the boy a dose of smallpox pus. It had no effect. Having had cowpox, the boy was protected against smallpox, a deadlier disease.

Pasteur guessed that something along the same line had happened to his chickens. The old culture, while unable to cause chicken cholera, was still in some way able to protect the chickens from catching the disease later. Pasteur experimented some more. He thought the key was leaving chicken cholera culture to sit out in the air for a prolonged time. This weakened the culture enough to make it safe.

Searching for an Anthrax Vaccine

Pasteur announced the discovery of a chicken cholera vaccine in 1880. He hoped his method would work to create vaccines for other diseases, too. In particular, he hoped it would work against anthrax.

You may be familiar with anthrax from more recent events. In 2001, anthrax spores—a deadly form of the anthrax microbe—were sent through the U.S. mail, infecting 22 people. In ordinary circumstances, anthrax is mainly a livestock disease.[3] In Louis Pasteur's day, the

Pasteur with two rabbits. The scientist used animals for many of his experiments on microbes and vaccines.

main concern was the cost to farmers when their animals became sick and died.

Pasteur had been studying anthrax since 1877, building on the findings of the German doctor Robert Koch. At the time, anthrax was a major killer of sheep. The French farmers lost millions of francs each year because of it. Shepherds had noticed that sheep that grazed in certain fields were more likely to get the disease. This was true even when the fields had been abandoned for years. Were the fields cursed?

Pasteur thought not. He knew that the shepherds usually buried dead animals in the fields where they had died. He also knew what Koch had found: the anthrax microbe has a hardy spore form that can survive for long periods without losing its ability to cause disease. Finally, Pasteur had seen signs of earthworms over the pits where animals were buried. He put these pieces together to solve the puzzle. Pasteur showed that earthworms were bringing the anthrax spores up from the pits to the surface of the soil. Animals who grazed there could then catch the disease.

The fields were not cursed. They just held bacteria. Armed with these facts, Pasteur offered his advice. He told shepherds either to burn dead animals or to bury them in spots where sheep and cattle would never graze.

By 1881, Pasteur had produced an anthrax vaccine. It was time to put this new vaccine to the test. Pasteur had always had a flair for the dramatic when it came to his work. Now he agreed to a public demonstration.

The Pouilly-le-Fort Affair

The historic anthrax test took place on a farm at Pouilly-le-Fort, a village southeast of Paris. On May 5, twenty-four sheep, six cows, and one goat were given Pasteur's vaccine against anthrax.[4] They were vaccinated again twelve days later. Then, on May 31, all of the vaccinated animals were injected with anthrax culture. So were twenty-four of the unvaccinated sheep, four unvaccinated cows, and one unvaccinated goat.[5]

This was the world's first public test of a vaccine made in a lab. Pasteur was not modest in his claims. He made the prediction that the vaccinated animals would all survive, while the unvaccinated animals would all sicken and die. Now there was nothing left to do but wait and see if his bold predictions would come true.

There were some tense moments the next day. What if Pasteur were wrong? It would be a disaster for his career. His fear, he told his wife and helpers, was that "this will be the ruin of all my work and of all my hopes!"[6]

On June 2, Pasteur returned to the farm to find out the results of his experiment. A crowd of more than two hundred officials, veterinarians, farmers, and others had already gathered there. Among them was a reporter from a London newspaper. Thanks to his widely read reports, the eyes of the world were on Pasteur that day.

When Pasteur arrived, the crowd burst into applause. His test had been a great success. All of the vaccinated animals were well, but twenty-one of the unvaccinated sheep and the lone unvaccinated goat were dead. The three remaining sheep who had been unvaccinated died by day's end, and the four unvaccinated cows all had a fever and swelling.

Pasteur's triumph appeared complete. Soon after the test, his lab began to make and sell anthrax vaccine to farmers and veterinarians. By the end of the century, millions of sheep and thousands of cows had been vaccinated.

Recently, doubt has been cast on some aspects of Pasteur's famous anthrax experiment. Pasteur had set out to make this vaccine by exposing the anthrax bacteria to oxygen in the air, the same way he had made the chicken cholera vaccine. His public statements implied that he had achieved his goal.

However, it now appears that Pasteur actually used another method for making the Pouilly-le-Fort vaccine. At the same time, a veterinarian named Jean-Joseph Henri Toussaint was also trying to develop an anthrax vaccine. Pasteur was eager to develop one first, so he rushed the news of his discovery.

At the time of the Pouilly-le-Fort experiment, much more work was still needed on Pasteur's oxygen-weakened vaccine. So Pasteur weakened the bacteria for this vaccine by using an antiseptic, a substance that slows or halts the growth of bacteria. This was the same method that the veterinarian Toussaint was already using in his research. Perhaps out of a desire to claim credit for an "original" discovery, Louis Pasteur hid the fact that he had made his vaccine with antiseptic as well.[7]

None of this changes the fact that Pasteur's vaccine worked better than his rival's. But it does show that his competitive nature got the better of him at times. By being less than honest in reports about his discovery, Pasteur broke one of the cardinal rules of science.

Yet despite this misstep, Louis Pasteur had shown that vaccines worked in livestock. Today, outbreaks of anthrax still occur in countries where livestock vaccination is not widely used. But anthrax is now rare in the United States and many other countries, thanks to widespread livestock vaccination.

11 Chapter

Victory Over Rabies

In Pasteur's day, infectious diseases took a terrible toll on human life. Little was known about how to prevent them. Pasteur wanted to change that. Even before his test of the anthrax vaccine, he had already chosen his next target. Pasteur aimed to make a vaccine against the deadly disease called rabies.

Rabies in humans has never been common. In the 1870s, it probably killed fewer than fifty people a year in France. Still, it has always inspired terror. People catch rabies from the bite of an infected animal, such as a dog, cat, ferret, raccoon, skunk, bat, fox, or coyote. The sick animal sometimes acts vicious and angry. The image of a "mad dog" attacking anyone in its path caught people's imagination and struck fear in their hearts. In fact, the word "rabies" comes from a Latin word meaning "to rage."

Death from rabies is a particularly unpleasant way to die. Inside the body, the disease attacks nerve cells. The first signs are often headaches, fever, and lack of energy. This is followed by confusion, restlessness, and anxiety. Next comes trouble sleeping, odd behavior, and thoughts that are out of touch with reality. By this point, untreated rabies is always fatal.[1]

Many diseases can only be prevented if a vaccine is given before a person comes into contact with the disease. Rabies is different. It develops slowly, usually taking a month or two from the time a person is bitten until the effects start. This delay means that there is enough time to give a vaccine after a person has already been bitten.

Developing a Rabies Vaccine

Pasteur began seriously studying rabies in 1880. He took the spinal cords of rabbits that had died of the disease. The spinal cord is the nerve tissue that runs through the backbone. Since rabies affects nerve tissue, the spinal cords carried the microbe that causes the disease. Pasteur stored these cords for two weeks in flasks full of clean, dry air. This made them almost harmless.

Pasteur had already studied a method of giving vaccines in a series of shots. If the microbes in a vaccine were not weakened enough, thcy could actually cause a disease rather than prevent it. However, if the microbes were not strong enough, the vaccine might not work. In Pasteur's studies of chicken cholera and anthrax, the animals had received a series of shots, starting with the weakest one and building up to the strongest. This let the animals gradually build up defenses against the disease.

In Pasteur's studies of rabies, healthy dogs were given several shots of dried spinal cord. The first shot contained cord that had been dried for the full fourteen days. It was too weak to make the dogs sick. The next shot contained cord that had been dried for a slightly shorter time and so was a little stronger. Each shot that followed was stronger still. Finally, the dogs were given shots of cord so fresh it should have caused the disease. But the dogs stayed healthy. The method of gradual vaccination had worked.

Pasteur was helped in his research by Émile Roux. The men needed a place to house the many animals used in their experiments. The city of Paris first let Pasteur have some land near his lab for this purpose. A few years later, Pasteur began using the old stables at Villeneuve l'Étang. This was a park in the village of Marnes-la-Coquette, located west of Paris. The stables were turned into a large dog kennel. A lab and living space were soon added, too.

Before long, Pasteur and his coworkers had successfully vaccinated fifty dogs. The next step was to try the vaccine in humans. But there was a catch: it was impossible to know for sure who would come down with rabies after a dog bite and who would not. If Pasteur waited until symptoms appeared, it was too late for the vaccine to work. But the unproven vaccine itself was risky. What if the vaccine actually made someone ill who would not have gotten sick otherwise? This was the ethical dilemma that Pasteur faced.

The First Human Patients

Then on July 6, 1885, three worried visitors came to see Pasteur. One was a nine-year-old boy named Joseph Meister. Two days before, Joseph had been attacked by a dog with rabies. He was bitten at least a dozen times. Joseph had deep wounds on his hands and legs, some so bad that he could barely walk. Joseph's mother and the dog's owner had brought the boy by train to Paris to seek Louis Pasteur's help.

Pasteur faced one of the toughest decisions of his life. Without the vaccine, Joseph might die. Pasteur thought he could probably save the boy, but he could not be sure. There was always a small risk that the vaccine would actually make matters worse.

Pasteur asked for advice from two doctors. After seeing the boy, they agreed that Joseph would likely develop rabies without the treatment. That is when Pasteur made up his mind. He had to try his best to save Joseph's life. Because Pasteur did not have a medical degree, he teamed up with a medical doctor who could treat the boy under Pasteur's watchful eye.

Later that same night, Joseph received his first shot of vaccine. Over the next eleven days, he was given twelve more shots, each slightly stronger than the one before. The last shot contained cord that had been taken just the day before from a rabbit that died of rabies. Afterward, Pasteur watched the boy anxiously for signs of the disease.

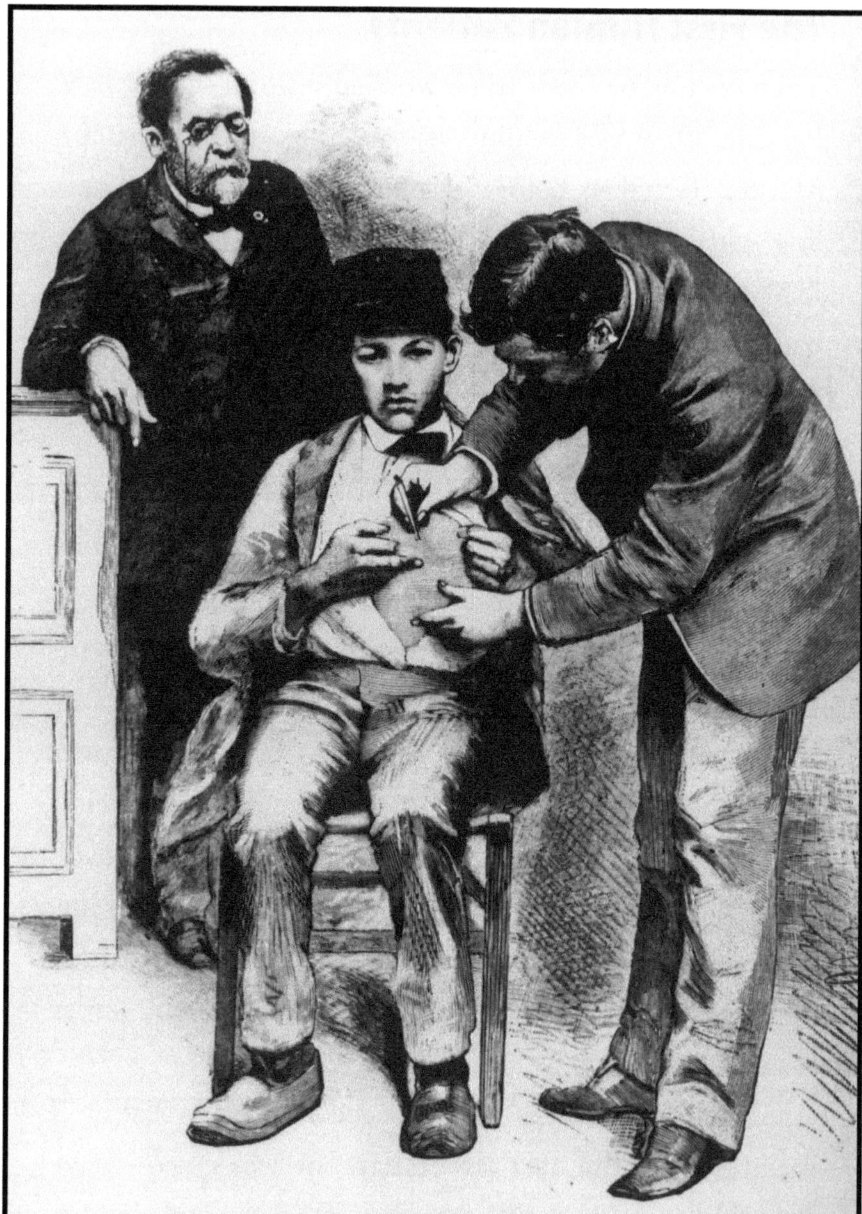

A drawing that appeared in a French magazine shows Pasteur watching as an assistant administers a shot of the rabies vaccine to Jean-Baptiste Jupille.

Pasteur was so worried that he had trouble sleeping through the night.

When Joseph returned home, Pasteur sent him stamped envelopes so that Joseph could write often. As the months passed, however, Pasteur's fears began to fade. The vaccine had worked! Joseph had escaped a horrible death.

In October, a second boy came to see Pasteur. He was Jean-Baptiste Jupille, a fifteen-year-old shepherd. Jean-Baptiste lived in a village near Arbois. The village mayor had written to Pasteur, telling him of the boy's bravery.

Jean-Baptiste and several younger shepherds had been watching over their sheep in a meadow when a dog with rabies attacked. Jean-Baptiste had rushed to protect the younger boys. He fought and killed the dog, but during the struggle, he was badly bitten. Without Pasteur's help, Jean-Baptiste seemed doomed.

Pasteur wrote back right away, offering to help Jean-Baptiste. The mayor put the boy on the next train to Paris. On October 20, Jean-Baptiste received his first shot of vaccine. But it was six days since the attack had occurred. Was the treatment too late? Once again, Pasteur spent many hours worrying. As before, though, the vaccine did its job. Jean-Baptiste stayed free of rabies.

A Hero Around the World

The world was thrilled by these dramatic successes against rabies. At age sixty-two, Pasteur had achieved his greatest fame yet. By October 1886, just fifteen months after

Joseph Meister's treatment, 2,500 people had received the rabies vaccine.

In fact, the demand was so great that it sometimes frustrated Pasteur, who would have liked more time to study the vaccine in his lab. Just months after Joseph and Jean-Baptiste received the vaccine, Pasteur wrote: "Already patients are rushing here from England, Russia, Hungary, Italy, and Germany. I would love to stop, but it is impossible. I would like to treat only recently bitten patients. Also impossible!"[2]

Not everyone was so impressed. At every stage of his career, Pasteur had faced some critics. This time was no different. Some people claimed that the rabies vaccine was useless or even dangerous.

Pasteur was forced to defend his treatment against these serious charges. His health suffered under the strain, and he began to show signs of heart trouble. In November 1886, his doctors sent him away from Paris for a period of rest.

At last, the English Commission on Rabies decided to resolve the controversy. In 1887, the commission presented its report. It found that Pasteur's new treatment had indeed saved many lives. This report did much to silence the critics.

Today people protect themselves and their pets against rabies by having their dogs and cats vaccinated. However, it is still possible to catch the disease from wild animals and unvaccinated pets. If a person is bitten by an animal that may be infected, a series of shots must still be given. But there have been big improvements since Pasteur's day.

Not so long ago, people who had been bitten by an animal with rabies had to get twenty-three painful shots in the abdomen. Today, rabies shots are less painful and work better. The first shot is given in the area of the bite. Then five more shots are given in the arm over a one-month period.[3]

Vaccines have now been developed to fight a number of other infectious diseases as well. Among them is typhoid fever, the illness that killed two of Louis and Marie Pasteur's daughters. Children today receive several kinds of vaccinations beginning soon after birth. As a result, some once-common diseases have become uncommon in many countries.

The greatest success of all has been achieved with smallpox. By the late 1970s, the disease itself had been completely wiped off the earth. Routine smallpox vaccination is no longer needed. However, the smallpox microbe still exists in labs, so the U.S. government keeps supplies of the vaccine on hand in case it is ever needed.[4]

12 Chapter

A Center for Science

People were grateful to Pasteur for developing the rabies vaccine. Patients from around the world flocked to his lab to get the new treatment. Money to fund his work also began to pour into Paris. Soon more than 2 million francs had been collected. This money was used to set up the Pasteur Institute in Paris. It was to be a center for the treatment and study of rabies and other problems in microbiology.

By 1888, the new institute was ready. A ceremony marking its opening was held on November 14. It was a grand occasion. Even the French president came. Pasteur had planned to give a short speech, but at the last minute, he was overcome by emotion. He asked his son, Jean-Baptiste, to read it instead.

In this speech, Pasteur thanked the people of the country he loved so deeply. Jean-Baptiste read: "Never has a

Frenchman addressing himself to other Frenchmen been more profoundly moved than I am at this moment."[1]

Founding the Pasteur Institute

Pasteur served as director of the Pasteur Institute until his death in 1895. Sadly, though, he was never able to do much research at the institute that bore his name. In October 1887, he suffered two small strokes. From that point on, his health and strength seemed to drain slowly away.

It was up to others to carry on the work Pasteur had begun. The next Pasteur Institute directors were Émile Duclaux and Émile Roux. These men had been two of Pasteur's closest coworkers. Now they were his allies in preserving the Pasteur name as a symbol of scientific greatness.

Over the years, eight Pasteur Institute scientists have been awarded Nobel Prizes in science. These are among the world's most prestigious science awards. Historically, Pasteur Institute scientists played key roles in learning about diseases such as rabies, plague, diphtheria, typhus, yellow fever, and polio. More recent advances have focused on diseases such as AIDS, hepatitis B, tuberculosis, ulcers, cervical cancer, genetic deafness, and tobacco addiction.

The main Pasteur Institute is still located in Paris. In addition, a worldwide network of twenty institutes is spread out over five continents. Among the sites are Algiers, Algeria; Phnom-Penh, Cambodia; Cayenne,

French Guyana; Athens, Greece; and Nouméa, New Caledonia.[2]

None of these institutes is located in the United States. However, there is a long tradition of cooperation between U.S. and Pasteur Institute scientists. Over the years, more than a thousand U.S. researchers have been welcomed at the Pasteur Institute. In return, hundreds of Pasteur scientists have come to the United States for advanced study and research.[3]

Pasteur received many honors late in life. Perhaps the most notable was a celebration on December 27, 1892, held at the Sorbonne on Pasteur's seventieth birthday. Pasteur, who was quite weak by this time, was led into the theater on the arm of the French president. The audience was filled with former students and assistants, officials, scientists, and other admirers.

Several speakers honored Pasteur's life and work. One was Joseph Lister, who told how Pasteur's writings had helped him revolutionize surgery. Addressing Pasteur, Lister said: "It is my great privilege to convey to you, tributes, thanks and respect from all involved in medicine and surgery; it is true to say that, of all people in the world today, medical sciences owe you the most."[4]

Pasteur himself was too ill to speak. Once again, his son read for him. He urged the young people in the crowd: "Live in the serene peace of laboratories and libraries."[5]

Le Petit Journal

SUPPLÉMENT ILLUSTRÉ

Huit pages : CINQ centimes

Le Petit Journal
CHAQUE JOUR 5 CENTIMES
Le Supplément illustré
CHAQUE SEMAINE 5 CENTIMES

ABONNEMENTS

	TROIS MOIS	SIX MOIS	UN AN
SEINE ET SEINE-ET-OISE	1 fr.	2 fr.	3 fr. 50
DÉPARTEMENTS	1 fr.	2 fr.	4 fr.
ÉTRANGER	1 50	2 50	5 fr.

Sixième année — DIMANCHE 13 OCTOBRE 1895 — Numéro 256

Though honored when he died in 1895, as he was here by this French publication, Pasteur was equally celebrated during his lifetime.

Fading Gently Away

Indeed, Pasteur had been happiest while working quietly in his lab. He told his assistants what to do, but he rarely shared his deeper thoughts with them. He liked for them to remain silent, too. He also discouraged outsiders from visiting the lab. Pasteur hated to be disturbed while he was busy.

As his body grew weaker with age, however, Pasteur's stern manner softened. People who knew Pasteur as an old man have said he appeared sad. His grandson, Pasteur Vallery-Radot, later described him this way: "I see again that face, that appeared to be carved from a block of granite—that high and large forehead, those grayish-green eyes, with such a deep and kind look . . . He seemed to me serious and sad."[6]

As death grew nearer, Pasteur became ever more tender toward his family. His daughter Marie-Louise and her husband lived nearby with their two children. Pasteur visited every afternoon. He took great joy in his grandchildren. In a note to his granddaughter, Camille Vallery-Radot, he wrote: "During these ten years, I believe, I never thought of you without loving you more and more."[7]

Pasteur's health continued to fail. In June 1895, he moved to Villeneuve l'Étang, where the dog kennel was located. There he would try to rest and recover, surrounded by his loved ones and the big trees of the park.

But Pasteur only grew worse. Speech became more and more difficult for Pasteur. His weakness and inability to move gradually increased. Finally, upon being offered a glass of milk, he said his last words: "I cannot."[8] Pasteur died late the next afternoon, on September 28, 1895. He was seventy-two years old.

A grand funeral was held for Pasteur on October 5. It was paid for by the French government. A church service was conducted at the famous Cathedral of Notre Dame in Paris. A distinguished crowd attended. Among those who came were the French president, a Russian grand duke, and a Greek prince.

After the church service, the crowd moved through the streets of Paris to the Pasteur Institute. Solemn throngs of ordinary people lined the way. They, too, wanted to pay their last respects to this national hero.

Pasteur's remains were first buried at the Cathedral of Notre Dame. Later they were transferred to a tomb in an elaborate chapel at the Pasteur Institute. The tomb is decorated in marble, gold, and colorful mosaics that picture some of Pasteur's discoveries. At the entrance are these words: "Blessed is the Man who Carries in his Soul a God, a Beautiful Ideal that he Obeys—Ideal of Art, Ideal of Science, Ideal of the Fatherland, Ideal of the Virtues of the Gospel."[9]

13 Chapter

Pasteur in the 21st Century

It has been more that a century since Pasteur's death, but his memory lives on in many ways. Throughout France, there are streets, schools, hospitals, and labs that bear the Pasteur name. In Paris, a major street is called Boulevard Pasteur, and a main subway station is called Station Pasteur. The University of Strasbourg, where Pasteur once taught chemistry, was split into three universities in the 1970s. The science and technology school is now known as University Louis Pasteur.[1]

The scientist's name has also been memorialized around the globe. A street in Ho Chi Minh City, Vietnam; a square in Tehran, Iran; and a main area in the city of Bandung, Indonesia: these are just a few of the places named for Pasteur. The scientist's namesakes even include craters on both the Moon and Mars.

Keeping the Memory Alive

In addition, several scientific terms are based on Pasteur's name. Pasteurization is the most familiar. The Pasteur effect is a blocking of fermentation that occurs when too much oxygen is present. A particular group of bacteria are known by the name Pasteurella, and the disease they cause is called pasteurellosis.

Pasteur's image can be seen in a variety of places as well. A statue of the great man stands in the courtyard of the Sorbonne. In the past, Pasteur's face also graced the five-franc bill and a French postage stamp. In addition, companies have put the famous scientist's name or image on a wide range of products, including beer, cheese, and disinfectant.

Of course, Pasteur's work holds a prominent place in the history of science and medicine. In addition, Pasteur's private life has been well documented. The house where he was born in Dôle, the family home in Arbois, the apartment where he lived at the Pasteur Institute, and the estate where he died at Marnes-la-Coquette have all been turned into museums.

Pasteur's life story has been retold many times. In 1900, his son-in-law, René Vallery-Radot, published a lengthy biography.[2] Several books by other authors followed. Even Hollywood was drawn to the drama of Pasteur's life. The result was a 1936 movie called *The Story of Louis Pasteur.* Actor Paul Muni won an Oscar for his lead performance in the film.[3]

Rethinking the Pasteur Legend

In recent years, though, Louis Pasteur's sterling reputation has become slightly tarnished. In 1995, Gerald Geison, a history professor, at Princeton University, well-known for his teaching and research on the history of medicine, published a biography titled *The Private Science of Louis Pasteur*. Based on close scrutiny of Pasteur's private lab notebooks, the book portrays Pasteur as far less perfect than his legend. The book points out times when Pasteur was not totally honest about his methods. It describes a complex man who could be difficult or spiteful, but who could also be noble and kind. [4]

It seems that Pasteur was no saint. Yet the list of his scientific achievements remains a very long and impressive one. He gave us pasteurization. He helped us understand how microbes cause disease. He also helped found the fields of stereochemistry and microbiology. In addition, Pasteur was a pioneer in the vaccination of humans and animals. The scientists who followed his lead made discoveries that have saved the lives of millions of people and spared many millions more from illness and suffering.

Pasteur was undeniably a great scientist. As a man, he had his flaws. But even his critics agree that Louis Pasteur devoted himself tirelessly to the welfare of humanity. This, above all else, is the reason he is still remembered and revered all over the world.

ACTIVITIES

IN PASTEUR'S FOOTSTEPS

Pasteur was always alert. This helped him see things that other people missed, such as the facets on crystals. It also helped him notice things that other people had seen but ignored, such as the behavior of bacteria under a microscope. By keeping your own eyes and mind open, you can follow in Pasteur's footsteps. Try these activities. Then answer the questions that follow.

CRYSTAL CLEAR

Examine the shapes of crystals for yourself. You can grow your own crystals easily by following these steps.

Materials needed:

- 6 pieces charcoal (the kind used for cooking outdoors)
- 6 tablespoons water
- 6 tablespoons laundry bluing
- 1 tablespoon ammonia
- 6 teaspoons salt
- a shallow pan

CAUTION: Laundry bluing and ammonia can be dangerous if they get in your eyes or on your skin. Have an adult help you with this experiment.

Procedure:

Put the charcoal pieces in the pan. Mix the water, bluing, ammonia, and salt. Then pour this mixture over the charcoal pieces. Place the pan in a warm spot so that the water dries up quickly.

Once the water has dried up, you should see crystals left behind. To get a better look at them, you can use a magnifying glass.

Questions:

What crystal shapes do you see? Can you draw the shapes the way Pasteur did? How accurate are your drawings?

YEAST FEAST

Yeast grows quickly in the presence of sugar. It causes the sugar to change into alcohol and the gas carbon dioxide.

Materials needed:

- 1 package of powdered yeast from the supermarket
- 1 tablespoon of sugar
- 2 cups of warm water
- a glass soda bottle
- a balloon

Procedure:

Mix the yeast and sugar in one cup of warm water. Make sure that the water is warm, not hot. Pour this mixture into the bottle. Then add the other cup of warm water. After squeezing any air out of the balloon, stretch its neck over the mouth of the bottle. Then set the bottle in a warm spot for three to four days, and watch what happens. Fermentation should soon cause some noticeable effects.

Check the bottle daily. You should see changes that are due to the presence of carbon dioxide, the same gas that causes bread to rise.

Questions:

Do you see bubbles being formed in the liquid? Is the balloon partly inflated? How do your answers change from day to day?

DIRTY TRICKS

You know that it is important to wash your hands before eating or cooking to keep from spreading microbes. This activity shows why.

Materials needed:

- 2 small potatoes
- a potato peeler
- 2 jars with lids that seal

The potatoes should be washed and the peeler and jars should be boiled to get rid of as many microbes on their surfaces as possible.

CAUTION: Boiling water is dangerous. Have an adult boil the peeler and jars. Leave air space at the top of the jars to collect gas produced during fermentation. Also, put the lids on loosely, which will allow some gas to escape. Otherwise, the jars might explode.

Procedure:

Leave your hands unwashed for several hours. Then peel one of the potatoes and put it in a jar. Wash the peeler. Next scrub your hands well. Then peel the other potato and put it in the other jar. Close both jars, taking care not to seal tightly. Label the first one "unwashed hands" and the second one "washed hands." Then leave both jars in a warm spot where they can be watched for several days.

Check the jars daily without removing their lids. After a few days, you will probably notice the growth of furry-looking mold on one or both potatoes. Mold grows from spores, special kinds of cells that are too small to be seen with the naked eye.

Questions:

Do you see furry-looking mold growing on the potato in the "unwashed hands" jar? In the "washed hands" jar? Which potato has more mold on it?

Your unwashed hands should have carried more mold spores than your washed hands. You could not see the spores on your dirty hands, any more than you can see the bacteria and other microbes there. But such microorganisms can still do harm. That is why it is important to wash your hands before handling food.

Chronology

1822—Louis Pasteur is born on December 27 to Jean-Joseph and Jeanne Pasteur in Dôle, France.

1827—Pasteur family moves to Arbois.

1839–42—Pasteur attends the Royal College of Besançon.

1842–43—Attends the Lycée Saint-Louis in Paris.

1843–48—Studies chemistry at the École Normale in Paris.

1847—Completes his Doctor of Science degree.

1848—Notes the differences between surfaces on two types of crystals. Jeanne Pasteur, Louis Pasteur's mother, dics.

1849–54—Pasteur teaches chemistry at the University of Strasbourg.

1849—Pasteur marries Marie Laurent on May 29 in Strasbourg.

1850—Daughter Jeanne is born.

1851—Son Jean-Baptiste is born.

1853—Daughter Cécile is born.

1854–57—Pasteur is dean of sciences at the University of Lille.

1857—Introduces his germ theory of fermentation.

1857–67—Serves as director of scientific studies at the École Normale.

1858—Daughter Marie-Louise is born.

1859—Daughter Jeanne dies.

1861—Pasteur discovers anaerobic bacteria.

1863–67—Teaches science at the École des Beaux-Arts in Paris.

1863—Daughter Camille is born.

1864—Pasteur gives famous lecture on spontaneous generation.

1865–69—Studies silkworm diseases in Alais.

1865—Conducts studies on pasteurization. Jean-Joseph Pasteur, Louis Pasteur's father, dies. Daughter Camille dies.

1866—Daughter Cécile dies.

1867–88—Pasteur is director of a chemistry lab at the École Normale.

1867–74—Teaches chemistry at the Sorbonne University in Paris.

1868—Suffers his first stroke.

1870–71—France is defeated in a war with Prussia.

1880—Pasteur announces the discovery of a chicken cholera vaccine.

1881—Conducts a public test of his anthrax vaccine at Pouilly-le-Fort.

1885—Joseph Meister receives the rabies vaccine in July. Jean-Baptiste Jupille receives the rabies vaccine in October.

1887—The English Commission on Rabies issues its report on the vaccine. Pasteur suffers two small strokes.

1888—The Pasteur Institute holds its opening ceremony on November 14.

1888–95—Pasteur is director of the Pasteur Institute in Paris.

1892—Pasteur is honored at the Sorbonne on his seventieth birthday.

1895—On September 28, Louis Pasteur dies at Villeneuve l'Étang, located Marnes-la-Coquette, at age seventy-two; his funeral is held on October 5.

Chapter Notes

Chapter 1. A Hero Is Born

1. Gerald L. Geison, *The Private Science of Louis Pasteur* (Princeton, N.J.: Princeton University Press, 1995), p. 22.
2. Ibid., p. 23.
3. Ibid., pp. 265–266.
4. Ibid., pp. 16–17.
5. Ibid., p. 40.

Chapter 2. Life at the Tannery

1. René Dubos, *Pasteur and Modern Science,* ed. Thomas D. Brock (Madison, Wis.: Science Tech, 1988), p. 7.
2. René Dubos, *Louis Pasteur: Free Lance of Science* (New York: Da Capo, 1960), xix.
3. Gerald L. Geison, *The Private Science of Louis Pasteur* (Princeton, N.J.: Princeton University Press, 1995), pp. 177–178.
4. René Vallery-Radot, *The Life of Pasteur,* trans. Mrs. R. L. Devonshire (Garden City, N.Y.: Doubleday, Page, 1927), pp. 11–12.

Chapter 3. The Call of Science

1. Pasteur Vallery-Radot, *Louis Pasteur: A Great Life in Brief,* trans. Alfred Joseph (New York: Alfred A. Knopf, 1970), p. 16.
2. René Vallery-Radot, *The Life of Pasteur,* trans. Mrs. R. L. Devonshire (Garden City, N.Y.: Doubleday, Page, 1927), p. 14.
3. Pasteur Vallery-Radot, p. 25.
4. René Vallery-Radot, pp. 21–22.
5. Ibid., p. 32.

Chapter 4. Gazing at Crystals

1. René Vallery-Radot, *The Life of Pasteur,* trans. Mrs. R. L. Devonshire (Garden City, N.Y.: Doubleday, Page, 1927), p. 39.
2. René Dubos, *Pasteur and Modern Science,* ed. Thomas D. Brock (Madison, Wis.: Science Tech, 1988), p. 19.
3. Ibid., p. 20.
4. Gerald L. Geison, *The Private Science of Louis Pasteur* (Princeton, N.J.: Princeton University Press, 1995), p. 25.
5. Pasteur Vallery-Radot, *Louis Pasteur: A Great Life in Brief,* trans. Alfred Joseph (New York: Alfred A. Knopf, 1970), p. 37.
6. Ibid., p. 39.
7. Geison, p. 139.

Chapter 5. The Beet Juice Problem

1. Pasteur Vallery-Radot, *Louis Pasteur: A Great Life in Brief,* trans. Alfred Joseph (New York: Alfred A. Knopf, 1970), p. 54.

Chapter 6. The Swan-Necked Flask

1. Pasteur Vallery-Radot, *Louis Pasteur: A Great Life in Brief,* trans. Alfred Joseph (New York: Alfred A. Knopf, 1970), p. 60.
2. René Dubos, *Louis Pasteur: Free Lance of Science* (New York: Da Capo, 1960), p. 177.

Chapter 7. From Grapes to Wine

1. Food and Drug Administration and National Science Teachers Association, "Food Safety A to Z Reference Guide," <http://www.cfsan.fda.gov/~dms/a2z-toc.html>.

Chapter 8. Saving the Silkworms

1. René Dubos, *Pasteur and Modern Science,* ed. Thomas D. Brock (Madison, Wis.: Science Tech, 1988), p. 91.
2. René Vallery-Radot, *The Life of Pasteur,* trans. Mrs. R. L. Devonshire (Garden City, N.Y.: Doubleday, Page, 1927), p. 118.
3. René Dubos, *Louis Pasteur: Free Lance of Science* (New York: Da Capo, 1960), p. 218.

4. Pasteur Vallery-Radot, *Louis Pasteur: A Great Life in Brief,* trans. Alfred Joseph (New York: Alfred A. Knopf, 1970), p. 92.

5. Gerald L. Geison, T*he Private Science of Louis Pasteur* (Princeton, N.J.: Princeton University Press, 1995), p. 30.

Chapter 9. The Tiniest Enemies

1. Alan G. Baxter, "Louis Pasteur's Beer of Revenge," Nature Reviews: Immunology, December 2001, vol. 1, pp. 229–232.

2. Pasteur Vallery-Radot, *Louis Pasteur: A Great Life in Brief,* trans. Alfred Joseph (New York: Alfred A. Knopf, 1970), p. 128.

3. René Dubos, *Pasteur and Modern Science,* ed. Thomas D. Brock (Madison, Wis.: Science Tech, 1988), p. 90.

Chapter 10. Warfare Against Germs

1. Bruno Latour, *The Pasteurization of France,* trans. Alan Sheridan and John Law (Cambridge, Mass.: Harvard University Press, 1988), pp. 69–70.

2. René Dubos, *Pasteur and Modern Science,* ed. Thomas D. Brock (Madison, Wis.: Science Tech, 1988), p. 111.

3. "Anthrax," *Centers for Disease Control and Prevention,* n.d. <http://www.bt.cdc.gov/agent/anthrax/> (December 21, 2006).

4. René Dubos, *Louis Pasteur: Free Lance of Science* (New York: Da Capo, 1960), p. 339.

5. Ibid., pp. 339–340.

6. Pasteur Vallery-Radot, *Louis Pasteur: A Great Life in Brief,* trans. Alfred Joseph (New York: Alfred A. Knopf, 1970), p. 150.

7. Gerald L. Geison, *The Private Science of Louis Pasteur* (Princeton, N.J.: Princeton University Press, 1995), pp. 145–176.

Chapter 11. Victory Over Rabies

1. "Rabies," *Centers for Disease Control and Prevention (CDC),* n.d. <http://www.cdc.gov/ncidod/dvrd/rabies/default.htm> (December 21, 2006).

2. Pim Allen, "Pasteur's Life and Pioneering Work," *The Lancet,* July 6, 2002, vol. 360, no. 9326, p. 93.

3. *Centers for Disease Control and Prevention (CDC),* "Rabies."
4. "Smallpox," *Centers for Disease Control and Prevention (CDC),* n.d. <http://www.bt.cdc.gov/agent/smallpox/> (December 21, 2006).

Chapter 12. A Center for Science

1. Gerald L. Geison, *The Private Science of Louis Pasteur* (Princeton, N.J.: Princeton University Press, 1995), p. 261.
2. "History," *Pasteur Institute,* n.d. <http://www. pasteur.fr/pasteur/histoire/histoireUS/Histoire.html> (December 21, 2006).
3. "Historical Relations with the United States," *Pasteur Foundation,* n.d.<http://www.pasteurfoundation.org/IP-USA.html> (December 21, 2006).
4. M. Schwartz, "The Life and Works of Louis Pasteur," *Journal of Applied Microbiology,* 2001, vol. 91, pp. 597–601.
5. Geison, p. 262.
6. René Dubos, *Louis Pasteur: Free Lance of Science* (New York: Da Capo, 1960), xxviii.
7. Pasteur Vallery-Radot, *Louis Pasteur: A Great Life in Brief,* trans. Alfred Joseph (New York: Alfred A. Knopf, 1970), p. 193.
8. Dubos, p. 57.
9. Pasteur Vallery-Radot, p. 197.

Chapter 13. Pasteur in the 21st Century

1. *University Louis Pasteur,* n.d. <http://www-ulp.u-strasbg.fr/en/bienvenue/> (December 21, 2006).
2. René Vallery-Radot, *The Life of Pasteur,* trans. Mrs. R. L. Devonshire (Garden City, N.Y.: Doubleday, Page, 1927).
3. *The Story of Louis Pasteur,* directed by William Dieterle, 1936. <http:find.allexperts.com/The_Story_of_Louis_Pasteur> (December 22, 2006).
4. Gerald L. Geison, *The Private Science of Louis Pasteur* (Princeton, N.J.: Princeton University Press, 1995).

Glossary

anaerobic bacteria—Bacteria that are active only when no oxygen is present.

anthrax—A disease that infects cattle, sheep, and goats and can be spread to humans.

antibiotic drug—A drug that works against diseases caused by bacteria or other microorganisms.

antiseptic—A substance that slows or halts the growth of bacteria.

applied science—The use of scientific knowledge to solve practical problems.

bacteria (singular: bacterium)—A broad group of microorganisms. Some bacteria cause disease, but many more are helpful to plants, animals, and humans.

crystal—One of the regularly shaped objects that many substances form when they harden.

culture—A colony of microorganisms grown in a lab for scientific study.

fermentation—A gradual chemical reaction in which sugar is changed into alcohol and carbon dioxide gas.

germ—A microbe.

germ theory—The theory stating that fermentation and certain diseases are caused by specific microorganisms.

immunology—The branch of science that studies the body's natural defenses against disease.

infectious disease—A disease caused by a microbe that can be spread from one living thing to another.

microbe—A microorganism that can cause disease.

microbiology—The branch of science that deals with microorganisms.

microorganism—A living thing too small to be seen without a microscope. Some microorganisms cause disease but others do not.

optical activity—The property of a substance to rotate in the direction which polarized light vibrates.

pasteurization—A process for heating milk or other liquids hot enough and long enough to kill harmful bacteria.

polarized light—Light that consists of orderly waves that vibrate in only one direction.

rabies—A deadly disease of the nervous system that is caused by a virus. People can get rabies from the bite of an infected animal.

silkworm—A moth larva that spins threads of silk to make a cocoon.

smallpox—A serious disease that produces a distinctive skin rash. This disease, which is caused by a virus, has been wiped out by vaccination.

spontaneous generation—The theory, now disproved, that living things arise from nonliving matter.

stereochemistry—The branch of science that deals with the position in space of tiny particles called atoms and how this position affects such things as optical activity.

sterilization—The act of making something free of microorganisms.

theory—An explanation based on observation and reasoning.

ultra-high-temperature (UHT) pasteurization—A form of pasteurization in which milk is heated between 138° and 150° C (280°–302° F) for one or two seconds. The milk is then packaged in germ-free, airtight containers.

ultrapasteurization—A form of pasteurization in which milk is heated to at least 138° C (280° F) for at least two seconds.

vaccine—A preparation of weakened or killed microbes that is given to a person or animal to prevent a disease.

virus—A type of disease-causing agent smaller than bacteria.

yeast—A one-celled mold that reproduces by budding.

Further Reading

Ackerman, Jane. *Louis Pasteur and the Founding of Microbiology.* Greensboro, N.C.: Morgan Reynolds, 2004.

Alphin, Elaine Marie. *Germ Hunter: A Story About Louis Pasteur.* Minneapolis: Carolrhoda, 2003.

Birch, Beverley. *Louis Pasteur: Father of Modern Medicine.* Woodbridge, Conn.: Blackbirch, 2001.

Collier, James Lincoln. *Vaccines.* New York: Benchmark Books, 2004.

Jakab, E. A. M. *Louis Pasteur: Hunting Killer Germs.* New York: McGraw-Hill, 2000.

Robbins, Louise E. *Louis Pasteur and the Hidden World of Microbes.* New York: Oxford University Press, 2001.

Silverthorne, Elizabeth. *Louis Pasteur.* San Diego, Calif.: Lucent Books, 2004.

Snedden, Robert. *Fighting Infectious Diseases.* Chicago: Heinemann Library, 2000.

INDEX

L

M

N

O

P

R

S

T

U

V

W

Y